Around the World

Homes

Margaret C. Hall

Heinemann Library
Chicago, Illinois

Designed by Lisa Buckley
Printed in Hong Kong

05 04 03 02 01
10 9 8 7 6 5 4 3 2 1

Library of Congress Cataloging-in-Publication Data
Hall, Margaret C., 1947-
   Homes / Margaret C. Hall.
      p. cm. -- (Around the world)
   Includes bibliographical references and index.
   ISBN 1-58810-103-7 (library binding)
   1. Dwellings--Juvenile literature. [1. Dwellings.] I. Title. II. Around the world
(Chicago, Ill.)

TH4811.5 .H35 2001
643.1--dc21
                                                    00-063270

Acknowledgments
The author and publishers are grateful to the following for permission to reproduce copyright material:
Demetrio Carrasco/Tony Stone, pp. 1, 10; Wolfgang Kaehler, pp. 4a, 5, 21, 26; Keren Su/Tony Stone, p. 4b;
Sharon Smith/Bruce Coleman, Inc., p. 4c; David Young-Wolff/Tony Stone, p. 6; Wendell Metzen/Bruce
Coleman, Inc., p. 7; David Hiser/Tony Stone, p. 8; Jean Dragen/Tony Stone, p. 9; Ric Ergenbright, p. 11; Horst
Baender/Tony Stone, p. 12; Lescourret/Explorer/Photo Researchers, p. 13; Jame Nelson/Tony Stone, p. 14; Bill
Bachmann/Photo Edit, p. 15; John Beatly/Tony Stone, p. 16; Patrick Rouillard/The Stock Market, p. 17; John
Warden/Tony Stone, p. 18; Jason Laure, p. 19; Kenneth Fink/Bruce Coleman, Inc., p. 20; Paul Chesley/Tony
Stone, p. 22; Vince Streano/Corbis, p. 23; Sue Cunningham/Tony Stone, p. 24; Adrian Murrell/Tony Stone, p.
25; Tony Stone, p. 27; Martha Cooper/Peter Arnold, p. 28; Nigel Hillier/Tony Stone, p. 29.

Cover: David Hiser/Tony Stone

Some words are shown in bold, **like this.** You can find
out what they mean by looking in the glossary.

Contents

People Have Needs

People everywhere have the same **needs**. They need food, clothing, water, and homes. They also need to be able to get from place to place.

Where people live makes a difference in what they eat and wear. It makes a difference in their homes and the kinds of **transportation** they use.

Why People Need Homes

Homes **shelter** people from the sun, wind, snow, and rain. They keep people warm in cold weather and cool in hot weather.

Homes give people a place to safely store their belongings. They are places where people can eat, sleep, and be together.

Homes Around the World

Homes are built in many sizes and shapes. They can be made from wood, bricks, **concrete**, or stone. They can even be made from mud, grass, or old tires.

People build homes to suit the **climate** in their part of the world. They use **resources** that grow or can be found where they live.

Homes for Cold Places

Some places get very cold in the winter. People who live in those places need homes that **shelter** them from the snow and wind.

People who live in cold **climates** need to keep warm. Their homes usually have furnaces or fireplaces. They may have thick walls and special windows to keep the heat inside.

Building Cold-Weather Homes

Thick forests grow in many cold **climates**. So wood is often used to build warm homes. Stone, brick, and **concrete** are other **construction** materials that are used.

In cold climates, there can be lots of snow. Cold-weather homes often have steep roofs with **overhangs**. The heavy snow and ice slide off the roof and away from the house.

Homes for Hot, Wet Places

In **tropical climates,** people need **shelter** from the sun, heat, and rain. They need houses that let air inside to cool things off.

Some homes in hot, wet places do not have walls. Others have **shutters** that keep out sun and rain but let in cool breezes.

Building Hot-Weather Homes

Many trees and plants grow in **tropical climates.** People often build their homes from wood. They may weave leaves or grasses together to make roofs.

Floods are common in areas that get a lot of rain. Sometimes houses are built on **stilts** to keep them above floodwaters. Being high off the ground makes the houses cooler, too.

Homes for Deserts

Deserts are very dry places. Days are usually hot, and nights can be cold. Desert people need homes that **protect** them from the sun, heat, wind, and cold.

Thick walls help desert homes stay
comfortable in hot and cold weather.
Houses are often built with open
courtyards in the middle. Courtyards
are cool, shady places on hot days.

Building Desert Homes

Few trees grow in **desert** areas. Desert
homes are not usually made from wood.
Because there is very little rain, they can
be made from things that would fall
apart in wet weather.

Some desert homes are made with mud walls and straw or grass roofs. Others are built out of adobe bricks. Adobe is a mixture of earth, straw, and clay that is dried in the sun.

Homes for Many People

In cities, there is not enough land for
every family to build a house of their own.
People share space by living in large
apartment buildings.

Sometimes people from many families
decide to live in a group and share a home.
Older people may live together so they
can be cared for by others.

Makeshift Homes

Sometimes people do not have enough money to buy regular **construction** materials. Instead, they build **makeshift** homes from things that have been thrown away.

Makeshift homes may be built from metal, cardboard, or scraps of wood. These homes do not have electricity or running water.

Homes that Move

Nomads move their **herds** to find fresh grass. They need homes that can go with them. They live in tents that can be folded and carried.

Other people live on the water, in houseboats. Sometimes their homes are also where they work. Some houseboats are like floating stores where other people buy things.

Special Homes

Earthships are houses that people build far from cities and towns. They are made with mud and old tires. Earthships are warm in winter and cool in the summer.

People make their homes in all kinds of
places. Some people even live in caves!
No matter what they look like, homes
shelter the people who live inside them.

Amazing Home Facts

✪ Long ago, people in some Arctic places lived in igloos—homes of snow and ice. People still build igloos for **shelter** on winter hunting trips. The rest of the time, they live in homes made of wood or other materials.

✪ Earthquakes are common in Japan. Many homes have lightweight sliding walls made from bamboo and paper. The lightweight walls move along with the earthquake. This helps to keep the house from breaking apart.

✪ Sometimes people share their houses with farm animals. In some mountain countries, families live on the second floor of the house. Their animals live on the first floor. Keeping the animals down below makes the upstairs warmer!

Glossary

apartment one of a number of living spaces in the same building

Arctic cold lands near the North Pole

climate year-to-year weather for an area

concrete man-made material that changes from a thick liquid to a rock-like solid

construction building

courtyard section of a building that is surrounded by walls but has no roof

desert dry place with very little rain

flood overflowing water

herd group of animals, such as sheep, cattle, or goats

makeshift something made without much planning from whatever can be found

needs things people must have in order to live

nomad person who spends his or her life moving from place to place instead of living in a permanent home

overhang slanted section of roof that sticks out past a house's walls

protect to keep safe

resource item available for use

shelter cover

shutter movable cover for a door or window

stilt post that supports a building above the ground or water

transportation ways people move from place to place

tropical place where the weather is hot and rainy

More Books to Read

Baker, Nicola. *Homes*. Danbury, Conn.: Children's Press, 1997.

Hewitt, Sally. *The Homes We Live In*. Austin, Tex.: Raintree Steck-Vaughn, 1997.

Jackson, Mike. *Homes Around the World*. Austin, Tex.: Raintree Steck-Vaughn, 1995.

Kalman, Bobbie. *Homes Around the World*. New York: Crabtree, 1994.

Index

10/8